!UOY ƎB Creative Innovators become mentally "STRONG"

Author
Roshanda D. Prior

Artwork

"Be You" Creative Innovators "STRONG"

This book is a must-have for anyone interested in self-awareness, personal development, and the role of Art in education. It is packed with activity pages, affirmations, inspirational quotes, and transformative creative exercises. These tools are designed to enhance your self-awareness, foster personal growth, and demonstrate the importance of Art in STEAM education. The book also equips you with lifelong learning skills.

Introducing the inaugural book in the 'Be You' Creative Innovators series, a collection of eight books designed to enhance your personal toolkit. Each book in the series focuses on a different aspect of personal development, providing you with a comprehensive guide to self-improvement and self-expression.

Join us in a collective endeavor to empower individuals and communities, harnessing the influence of arts in education, economics, health/wellness, safety, and agriculture/natural resources. This is not just an opportunity for growth; it's a chance to make a difference TOGETHER.

YOU can make a difference one person at a time, starting with YOURSELF!

Roshanda PRIOR

Roshanda Denise Prior ABA, BFA, MA
copyright 2024

MENTALLY STRONG

Be Strong...You are Strong...I am Strong... Become Strong

**Inspired by
Issachar
Miracle
Jerusalem**

Table of contents

Introduction

Hello! My name is "STRONG"!

What an honor! You have been CHOSEN to receive the empowering life tools in this book. Yes, YOU are the only one of its kind, an ORIGINAL. Improving a better you is a better society for everyone. "Be You Creative Innovators" series, has garnered popularity, high demand, and integration into education, team-building, sensitivity training, ministry, and workshops. This is not only an excellent book to read, but the valuable life tools implemented will activate and/or improve the greatness in being mentally strong already in you. Everyone's mental strength is demonstrated in their unique character. Our book family vision is to help humanity become mentally stronger. Our community mission is" BE YOU," which means being true to yourself by embracing and accepting your inside/outside beauty, both mentally and physically. The inside beauty is the joyful vibration of goodness, positivity, and self-love. The outer beauty is being unapologetic and proud of your attributes, features, talents, and uniqueness without being influenced or defined by society. Live the best life by representing the one-of-a-kind masterpiece you were created to be."
 Roshanda D. Prior

Let us embark on a limitless life journey together. This book is a timeless treasure meant to be passed down through generations. Life is a constant flow of new people, things, places, and situations, spanning your past, present, and future. Every moment holds significance. The book comprises transformative insight and interactive exercises designed to flex your mental STRONG muscle– a metaphor for your resilience and inner strength– that is ready to be activated in your life NOW!

Look in the mirror
RECREATE yourself...
REIMAGINE yourself mentally...
STRONG!

STRONG

WHAT is mentally strong?

WHAT is mentally strong? It is practicing, developing, challenging, and living in a healthy mental mindset during all changes that will be acquired in life. It is the ability to care for and maintain a healthy lifestyle mentally, spiritually, physically, and financially. It is the ability to persevere during daily changes, unexpected challenges, and trauma. Mentally strong individuals not only survive adversity, they thrive on it. They learn, grow, and strive to process negative and positive information from the world around them and from within. Conquering and maintaining a healthy mindset during life's inevitable ups and downs becomes a beacon of hope. It's about taking care of yourself mentally and physically and being intentional about your emotional growth. There is no other option. It is seeking positive outcomes, support and using proactive coping skills. You take charge of your thoughts and destiny and embrace every error and challenge as a learning opportunity to become an example of a winner in your one-lane race. You are emotionally charged to be resilient, believe in yourself, rule your emotions, gain self-empowerment, and stay flexible. Mentally strong individuals turn roadblocks into opportunities by learning from their mistakes. Being mentally strong is a daily skill that can be applied in both personal and professional life, and it involves seeking positive outcomes and support using proven strategies. Being mentally strong is not when a problem arises that you then become isolated, outraged, indulge in drugs, addictions, overeating, bullying, self-pity, or allowing others to control your emotions. You can, will, and BECOME one of those mighty mentally STRONG individuals! Everyone is born capable of living a successful, joyful, and productive life.

Life is full of events, situations, challenges, and obstacles. Although they may influence your future, remember you have the power to control and produce a positive outcome. It's time to say goodbye to sadness, anger, hopelessness, depression, and unnecessary anxieties. Say hello to an uplifting, optimistic mindset that will lead you to a life of positive actions. Yes, your life will have ups and downs, but with these life tools, which can include strategies like positive self-talk, mindfulness, and goal setting, you can make the most of the ups. You have the strength within you to do it! Are you ready to build your mental muscles and get them pumping? Let's learn and execute how to flex those inner cognitive strengths!

WHAT MAKES ME MENTALLY STRONG?

"Walk by FAITH with or without
your socks or shoes"
Donald L. Fulbright Jr

"Sometimes you just have to sit in that thinking chair until
you come up with a plan. and remember that you sat in that
thinking chair alone. Now go and ACHIEVE that plan."
Ur Saviour R. Branch

"The race isn't easy but the finish line is beautiful. Meaning
whatever journey you take in life there will be trails and
tribulations that you face but once you get to where you
are destined , only the BEST is yet to come."
"Millie" Johnson

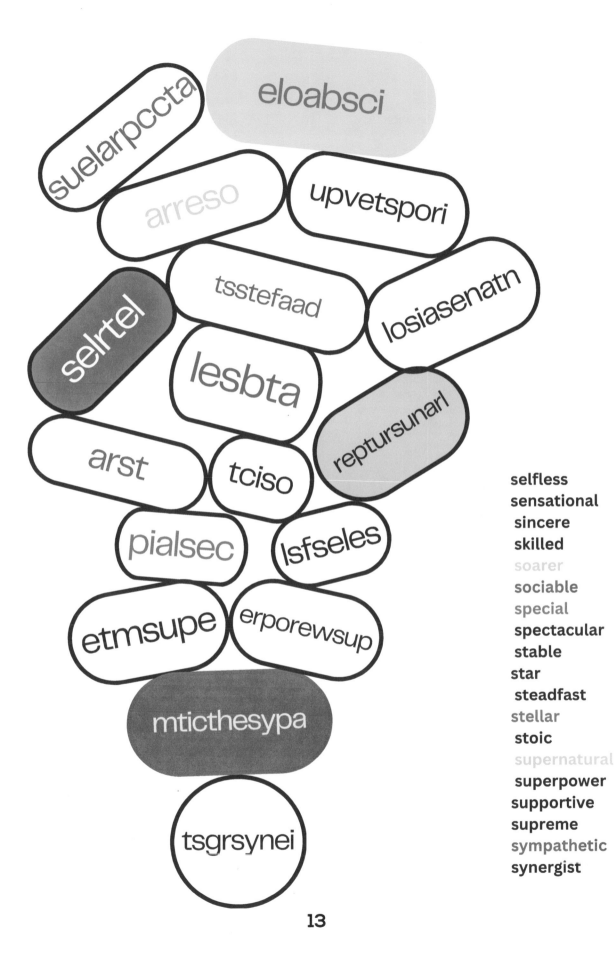

suelarpccta

eloabsci

arreso

upvetspori

tsstefaad

losiasenatn

selrtel

lesbta

reptursunarl

arst

tciso

pialsec

lsfseles

etmsupe

erporewsup

mticthesypa

tsgrsynei

selfless
sensational
sincere
skilled
soarer
sociable
special
spectacular
stable
star
steadfast
stellar
stoic
supernatural
superpower
supportive
supreme
sympathetic
synergist

Words have POWER! You have that inner power already. Think, Say, and activate with your ACTIONS! Let's LEARN and GROW!

SELFLESS
–concerned more with the needs and wishes of others than with one's own; unselfish.

SENSATIONAL
–very good indeed; very impressive or attractive.

SINCERE
–saying what they genuinely feel or believe; not dishonest or hypocritical.

SKILLED
–having or showing the knowledge, ability, or training to perform a certain activity or task well.

SOARER
–to ascend to a higher or more exalted level to rise to majestic stature

SOCIALABLE
–willing to talk and engage in activities with other people; friendly.

SPECIAL
–better, greater, or otherwise different from what is usual.

SPECTACULAR
–beautiful in a dramatic and eye–catching way.

STABLE
–not likely to give way or overturn; firmly fixed.

STAR
– is a beacon of hope, a shining light that guides the way. It's a symbol of positivity.
Happiness and renewal

STEADFAST
–the person will calmly hold firm to the chosen position and follow through with determination.

STELLAR
–outstanding, wonderful, better than everything else, a word of praise or excitement.

STOIC
–determined not to complain when going through hardships. Focusing on things that one can control.

SUPERNATURAL
–attributed to some force beyond scientific understanding or the laws of nature

SUPERPOWER
–flight, superhuman strength and speed, invulnerability or psionics.

SUPPORTIVE
–providing encouragement or emotional help. You are kind and helpful to someone at a difficult or unhappy time in their life.

SUPREME
–highest in rank or authority; paramount; sovereign; chief

Knowing yourself starts with thinking and expressing what is essential. Begin by stating your name and then affirm with "I AM."

I _____ embody the following qualities:

- I am SELFLESS, prioritizing the needs and desires of others over my own, showing unselfishness.

- I am SENSATIONAL, imposing, and attractive.

- I am SINCERE, always expressing genuine feelings and beliefs, avoiding. dishonesty or hypocrisy.

- I am SKILLED, possessing the knowledge, ability, and training to excel in various activities or tasks.

- I am ascending to higher levels and achieving majestic stature.

- I am SOCIABLE, friendly, and willing to engage in conversations and activities with others.

- I am SPECIAL, different, and greater than usual.

- I am SPECTACULAR, stunningly beautiful in a dramatic and eye-catching manner.

- I am stable, firmly fixed, and not likely to give way or overturn.

- I am a STAR, a beacon of hope and positivity, guiding the way with happiness and renewal.

- I am STEADFAST, maintaining a firm position with determination.

- I am STELLAR, outstanding, and praiseworthy, surpassing everything else with excitement.

- I am STOIC, enduring hardships without complaint and focusing on what can be controlled.

- I am SUPERNATURAL, connected to forces beyond scientific understanding. or natural laws.

- I am a SUPERPOWER, possessing abilities like flight, superhuman strength, and invulnerability.

- I am SUPPORTIVE, offering encouragement and emotional assistance to those in need during difficult times.

- I am SUPREME, holding the highest rank or authority, paramount, sovereign, and chief.

New mindset, New directions,
New narrative, New creation,
NEW BEGINNINGS...

I embody selflessness, characterized by a genuine concern for the needs and desires of others and prioritizing well-being by displaying unselfish traits. I am known for being sensational, denoting an exceptional level of excellence. My sincere expression of thoughts and beliefs is exhibited through genuine expression, always transparent, honest, and without deceit or insincerity. I possess a high skill level and demonstrate proficiency in various activities or tasks, showcasing knowledge, ability, and aptitude. As a soarer, I aspire to elevate myself to greater heights, reaching a more exalted level and attaining a majestic stature. Being sociable, I am friendly and engaging, readily interacting with others and participating in social activities. I am considered unique, distinctively better, more significant, or otherwise distinctive. My presence is described as spectacular, radiating beauty in a dramatic and visually striking manner. Stability characterizes me, reflecting a firm and unwavering nature resistant to upheaval. Like a bright star, I serve as a beacon of hope, illuminating the way with positivity, happiness, and rejuvenation. In my steadfastness, I exhibit an unwavering determination to maintain my stance and see-through commitments with steadfast perseverance. Renowned for my stellar qualities, I am recognized for being outstanding, exceptional, and superior in comparison to others, evoking praise and excitement. Embodying a stoic attitude, I face hardships without complaint, focusing on elements within my control. The supernatural is attributed to me, symbolizing forces beyond scientific understanding or the laws of nature. Possessing superpowers akin to flight, superhuman strength and speed, or invulnerability, I exhibit extraordinary abilities. My supportive nature is not just a trait; it's a commitment. I always provide encouragement and emotional assistance to others during challenging or distressing times. Regarded as supreme, I hold the highest rank or authority, standing as paramount, sovereign, and chief in various aspects.

Start by affirming and creating statements that acknowledge your inherent qualities. Embrace and believe the truth about yourself now and work towards building a positive future.

■ I am _____ and I

_____

_____

_____

■ I am _____ and I

_____

_____

_____

I am _____ and I

I am _____ and I

_____

_____

I am _____ and I

_____

_____

I am _____ and I

I am   and I

I am   and I

I am   and I

I am   and I

YOU ARE STRONG

WHY you are mentally strong?

Your "WHY" for being mentally strong is to make the right choices with excellent outcomes. But even if you make the wrong choice, you can redeem your life by self-correction, learning, growing, and making a different decision for your future. WHY you are mentally strong is because you chose to execute regardless of the outcome there is no stagnation. Managing your mental patterns can be learned and taught, but you will always be the one who lives within you. Being mentally strong when you have the revelation to know may seem hard now, but if you do not change your MINDSET, it will be even harder later. Every human, including you, has the potential for resilience. You possess one mind, body, soul, and spirit, regardless of your physical or mental status. This is a fact. You were not born as a weak, defeated, hopeless individual. It is only because your surroundings have affected your thinking as you have lived. Some may have been in a better environment than others, but regardless, it does not remove the fact that you were born strong. The ultimate distinction between the two is the choices. This is why you can hear about the lives of people who grew up in poverty, were in single-parent households, had no parents, and had severe health conditions but still persevered to live healthy, productive, and prosperous lives. Their resilience in the face of adversity is a testament to the strength we all possess. Those are options that everyone will have throughout their life. The inner self is sometimes known as intuition; you know something is wrong or right but cannot explain how you came to that conclusion. Once you have been exposed to wisdom, knowledge, and understanding, there is no excuse for not deciding to be mentally strong and make impactful decisions. Your thinking, focus, and attention are less destructive. It reduces the downward spirals of self-pity and self-criticism that lead to mental illness. There will be memories of the past or trauma that will arise suddenly to take your focus. It is not if these memories will happen but when. It could be something you see, hear, or feel, but this is normal for everyone.

You have the power to process the thoughts and decide what to filter in or out. Ask yourself the question How does this benefit me? Is this helping me to advance or adding value to my life? If not, terminate and disconnect from those thoughts. Replace them by reimagining a better situation and outcome for your future. This will give you a sense of control. The reality is no one will ever have complete control over their lives. For instance, there are car accidents, airplane crashes, injuries, arguments, sickness, school, family, and business disappointments that you did not expect.

Why me? Why not you?

_____

_____

_____

_____

_____

_____

_____

_____

_____

_____

_____

_____

Oh nothing....Love you
Conley H. Penn Jr

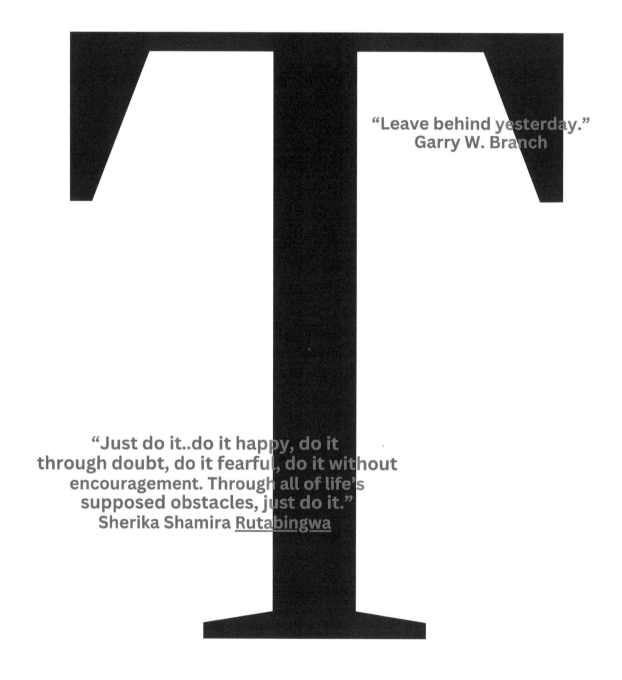

"Leave behind yesterday."
Garry W. Branch

"Just do it..do it happy, do it
through doubt, do it fearful, do it without
encouragement. Through all of life's
supposed obstacles, just do it."
Sherika Shamira Rutabingwa

lbotorutsheero

edattnle

psennarattr

ronaemrsfrt

labeahcet

caehtreh

icsneatuo

nkhtufla

nedrstetrte

nirehtk

zaiarertllb

suortwehtyt

ulatftc

munatphitr

mileyt

recitrfi

aeneteredhrdt

npcothot

mayapeerlt

oouhthrg

tactful
talented
teachable
teacher
teamplayer
tenacious
tenderhearted
terrific thankful
thinker
thorough timely
topnotch
trailblazer
transformer
transparent
trendsetter
triumphant
troubleshooter
trustworthy

23

TACTFUL
- honest; fair; straightforward. Clever

TALENTED
- having a natural aptitude or skill for something.

TEACHABLE
-capable of being taught. especially : able and willing to learn.
teacher-a person who teaches

TEAMPLAYER
-person who plays or works well as a member of a team or group.

TENACIOUS
- persistent, Not easily dispelled

TENDERHEARTED
-having a kind, gentle sentimental nature

TERRIFIC
-extraordinarily good or great

THANKFUL
-taking a moment to reflect how grateful you are

THINKER
- A person who thinks deeply and seriously

THROUGH
- complete with regard to every detail; not superficial or partial.

TIMELY
-done or occurring at a favorable or useful time; opportune.

TOPNOTCH
- the highest quality; excellent.

TRAILBLAZER
- pioneer; an innovator.

TRANSFORMER
-person or thing that transforms something.

TRANSPARENT
- having thoughts, feelings, or motives that are easily perceived.

TRENDSETTER
- having the effect of starting or helping to popularize a new trend, fashion, style, or movement

TRUIMPHANT
- having won a victory or mastered a difficulty.

TROUBLESHOOTER
-person whose job is to solve major problems or difficulties

TRUSTWORTHY
-able to be relied on as honest or truthful.

I   embody the following qualities

- I am discreet – honest, fair, straightforward. Clever
- I am talented– having a natural aptitude or skill for something.
- I am teachable –capable of being taught. Especially: able and willing to learn.
- I am a teacher–a person who teaches
- I am a team player, a person who plays or works well as a member of a team or group.
- I am Tenacious– persistent, Not quickly dispelled
- I am tenderhearted –have a kind, gentle, sentimental nature
- I am terrific –extraordinarily good or great
- I am thankful –taking a moment to reflect on how grateful you are
- I am a thinker – A person who thinks deeply and seriously
- I am thorough – complete about every detail, not superficial or partial.
- I am timely –done or occurring at a favorable or advantageous time; opportune.
- I am top–notch– the highest quality; excellent.
- I am a trailblazer – pioneer, and innovator.
- I am a transformer, a person or thing that transforms something.
- I am transparent – having thoughts, feelings, or motives that. they are easily perceived.
- I am Trendsetter– having the effect of starting or helping to popularize a new trend, fashion, style, or movement.
- I am triumphant– having won a victory or mastered a difficulty.
- I am a troubleshooter whose job is to solve significant problems. problems or difficulties.
- I am trustworthy and able to be relied on as honest or truthful.

New mindset, New directions, New narrative, New creation, NEW BEGINNINGS.....

Exemplifying a more formal demeanor, I embody tactfulness, characterized by a blend of honesty, fairness, and directness, complemented by astuteness. Furthermore, my innate talent manifests as a natural proficiency and skill across various domains. An essential facet of my character is my teachability, marked by a receptiveness to instruction and a keen eagerness for learning.

As a leader, I not only impart knowledge and guidance but also embody the essence of a collaborative team player adept at working within group dynamics. My resilience and persistence underscore my tenacious disposition, revealing a steadfast resolve to face challenges.

Additionally, my compassionate nature reflects a gentle and kind-hearted sentiment, while my overall demeanor is characterized by exceptional qualities, denoting a remarkable presence. Cultivating gratitude is a significant practice for me, as I regularly pause to appreciate the aspects of life that merit thankfulness.

My intellectual inclination leans toward profound contemplation and a meticulous and detail-oriented approach to all endeavors. I strive to act promptly, seizing opportune moments for decisive action.

Maintaining a commitment to excellence, I consistently strive for top-notch quality and set high standards for myself. Embracing the role of an innovator, I pioneer novel ideas and techniques, effecting transformative change and evolution across various spheres.

Transparency is a cornerstone of my character; my thoughts, emotions, and intentions are readily apparent. As a trendsetter, I play a pivotal role in initiating and popularizing new trends, styles, or movements.

In navigating challenges, I emerge victorious, conquering obstacles and achieving triumphs. Proficient in troubleshooting, I adeptly navigate complex problems and hurdles. Central to my character is unwavering trustworthiness, reflecting a steadfast commitment to reliability, honesty, and truthfulness in all pursuits.

Start by affirming and creating statements that acknowledge your inherent qualities. Embrace and believe the truth about yourself now and work towards building a positive future.

■ I am   and I

_____

_____

_____

■ I am   and I

_____

_____

_____

I am   and I

> Craft a declaration defining who you are presently or aspire to be in the future. Express your qualities, gifts, talents, and aspirations in this statement. Remember, there is always more to discover about yourself, so continue to write your vision!

I am   **and I**

_____

_____

_____

I am   **and I**

_____

_____

_____

I am   **and I**

I am   and I

I am   and I

I am   and I

I am   and I

BECOME STRONG

HOW to be mentally strong in you

HOW to be mentally strong will require you to be intentional and persistent. The critical foundation for learning mental strength lies in focus, determination, and execution. As individuals, we gain the necessary insights and develop skills to overcome the most challenging demands of life when we become aware of our negative mental status. Your unique approach is essential to give you full access to your blueprint and authentic self in every way possible. Unexpected setbacks and disappointments are a part of life; despite life's inevitable conflicts, Mental strength fosters resilience and confidence, enabling you to weather the most challenging storms and achieve your goals and dreams. The longer you live, plans and situations are subject to change. It is common for us to have made grievous and shameful mistakes in the past. No matter the mistakes, self-condemnation and self-hatred are not helpful and lead to unproductivity. Mentally strong individuals understand that everyone makes mistakes, and instead of dwelling on past failures, they use them as opportunities for growth. This approach will help you remain calm, collected, and in control of your emotions. Developing your mental strength is the ultimate foundation that will catapult you forward. It is obtainable through consistent practice and discipline. Remaining realistic and avoiding making decisions out of anger, urgency, or anxiety is crucial. Instead, take the time to think through your response to those unexpected obstacles. When faced with demanding situations, evaluating the facts and responding thoroughly and thoughtfully is essential. Love yourself enough to grow from experience and challenges because it is a learning curve that everyone will navigate. Remain confident, determined, and focused despite the most intense pressure. Educate yourself by seeking information via self-help books, family, positive peers, or professional help. This knowledge is your power, but it's only effective when you PUT IT INTO PRACTICE. No matter what happens, never quit, and always strive to move forward toward your goals and dreams. Believe in yourself and never compare yourself to others. Be the BEST version of you!

How are you doing???

Born GREAT
Rashad D. Penn

"Life teaches us through every challenge; it's in OVERCOMING them that we find our true strength."
Haily Fulbright

"Do not let unkind words define you. Remember, you are someone SPECIAL."
Ivy Estelle

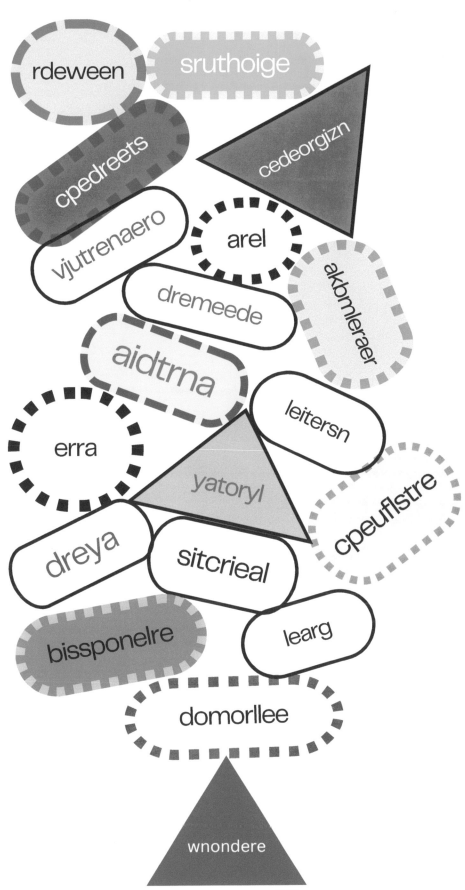

rdeween

sruthoige

cpedreets

cedeorgizn

vjutrenaero

arel

dremeede

akbmleraer

aidtrna

erra

leitersn

yatoryl

cpeuflstre

dreya

sitcrieal

learg

bissponelre

domorllee

wnondere

radiant
rare
ready
real
realistic
recognized
redeemed
regal
rejuvenator
remarkable
renewed
renowned
resilient
respected
respectful
responsible
righteous
rolemodel
royalty

Words have POWER! You have that inner power already. Think, Say, and activate with your ACTIONS! Let's LEARN and GROW!

RADIANT
- sending out light.. Shining or glowing brightly

RARE
-not found in large numbers and consequently of interest or value.

READY
-a suitable state for an activity, action, or situation; fully prepared

REAL
-not imitation or artificial genuine.

REALISTIC
-having or showing a sensible and practical idea of what can be achieved or expected.

RECOGNIZED
- acknowledge the existence of Validity

REDEEMED
- gain or regain possession of something in exchange for payment
Compensation for faults

REGAL
- magnificent or dignified

REJUVENATOR
- someone or something that gives a new vigor, restores to an original or
new state, renews and refreshes

REMARKABLE
- worthy of attention

RENEWED
-worthy of being or likely to be noticed especially as being uncommon or extraordinary

RENOWN
-widely acclaimed and highly honored : celebrated.

RESELIENT
-implies the ability to recover shape quickly when the deforming force or pressure is removed. the process and outcome of successfully adapting to difficult or
challenging life experiences, especially through mental, emotional, and behavioral flexibility and adjustment to external and internal demands.

RESPECTED
-admired, correct in character or behavior, worthy of honor and respect

RESPECTFUL
-show consideration and regard for someone or something

responsible
-having a capacity for moral decisions and therefore accountable; capable of rational thought or action:

RIGHTEOUS
-morally right or justifiable and virtuous

ROLE MODEL
-person looked to by others as an example to be imitated.

ROYALTY
-the rank, status, or power of a king or queen; royal position, dignity, sovereignty

Knowing yourself starts with thinking and expressing what is essential.

Begin by stating your name and then affirm with "I AM."

I, _____ embody the following qualities:

- I am radiant, emitting light and shining brightly.
- I am rare, unique, and valuable due to scarcity.
- I am ready and fully prepared for any activity or situation.
- I am honest, genuine, and not artificial.
- I am realistic, possessing a practical view of achievable goals.
- I am recognized, acknowledging validity and existence.
- I am redeemed, regaining possession through compensation.
- I am regal, exuding magnificence and dignity.
- I am a rejuvenator, revitalizing and refreshing to an original or new state.
- I am remarkable and deserving of attention.
- I am renewed, uncommon, or extraordinary, likely to be noticed.
- I am renowned, celebrated, and widely acclaimed.
- I am resilient and able to recover quickly from challenging experiences.
- I am respected, admired, and worthy of honor.
- I am respectful and show consideration for others.
- I am responsible, accountable, and capable of rational decisions.
- I am righteous, morally justifiable, and virtuous.
- I am a role model, someone others look up to as an example to follow.

I emanate brilliance, a rare quality that radiates light and captivates attention. Preparedness, a vital trait, ensures readiness for any endeavor. Authenticity, the paramount virtue, distinguishes the genuine from the artificial, setting one apart. A realistic approach entails practical expectations and achievable goals. Being recognized acknowledges one's existence and validity. Redemption involves regaining possession through compensation. Regality exudes magnificence and dignity. A rejuvenator revitalizes, renews, and refreshes to an original state. Remarkable qualities draw attention and admiration. Renewed attributes are noteworthy and uncommonly extraordinary. Renowned individuals are widely celebrated and honored. Resilience denotes the ability to rebound swiftly from adversity, adapting to life's challenges with mental, emotional, and behavioral flexibility. Respect is earned through admirable conduct and character. Being respectful demonstrates consideration and esteem. Responsibility entails moral accountability and rational decision-making. Righteousness embodies moral justification and virtuousness. A role model serves as an exemplary figure for others to emulate. Royalty symbolizes kings and queens' regal status, power, and dignity.

Start by affirming and creating statements that acknowledge your inherent qualities. Embrace and believe the truth about yourself now and work towards building a positive future.

■ I am _____ and I

_____

_____

_____

■ I am _____ and I

_____

_____

_____

I am _____ and I

Craft a declaration defining who you are presently or aspire to be in the future. Express your qualities, gifts, talents, and aspirations in this statement. Remember, there is always more to discover about yourself, so continue to write your vision!

I am _____ and I

_____

_____

_____

I am _____ and I

_____

_____

_____

I am _____ and I

I am _____ and I _____

I am _____ and I _____

I am _____ and I _____

I am _____ and I _____

I AM STRONG

WHO is the mental strong?

The 'WHO' is you! It's been you all this time. To embark on this journey of personal growth, you must think STRONG, accept, embrace, believe, and demonstrate STRONG. YOU DESERVE IT! Everything you were born to do is NOW and waiting for you to EXECUTE. Have you ever felt as though there is an emptiness inside? or have you never been good enough or satisfied from within? It is because, as humans, our lives will demonstrate emotional roller coasters, such as feeling unfulfilled or lacking confidence that we are not operating to our fullest potential. Please do not settle for temporary lies. It is not your permanent destination. Choose the truth or the lie. The truth will reveal a brighter future, and the lie will become mental bondage. This inner mental strength is wanting to live! All of YOU, not just some of you, but the complete phenomenal individual you were born to BE!

Remember, mental strength is not about being perfect or always having it together. It's about YOUR RESILIENCE, determination, and the ability to bounce back from challenges. It's about embracing your uniqueness, believing in yourself, and pursuing your dreams. You have the power within you to overcome any obstacle and achieve greatness. So, stand tall, stay positive, and keep moving forward confidently. You are stronger than you think and have the strength to conquer anything that comes your way. Embrace your inner strength and unleash the incredible potential that lies within you. You can achieve amazing things, and the world is waiting for you to shine bright. Believe in yourself, trust your abilities, and let your mental strength guide you to SUCCESS!

Reflection notes

"Self-love is genuine LOVE."
Sonya L. Johnson

"Tell me something GOOD."
Jerry Santana Branch
B.A. Psy, M.A. CART. LCDC

"Success is not a destination,
it's a DECISION."
Eric Stovall

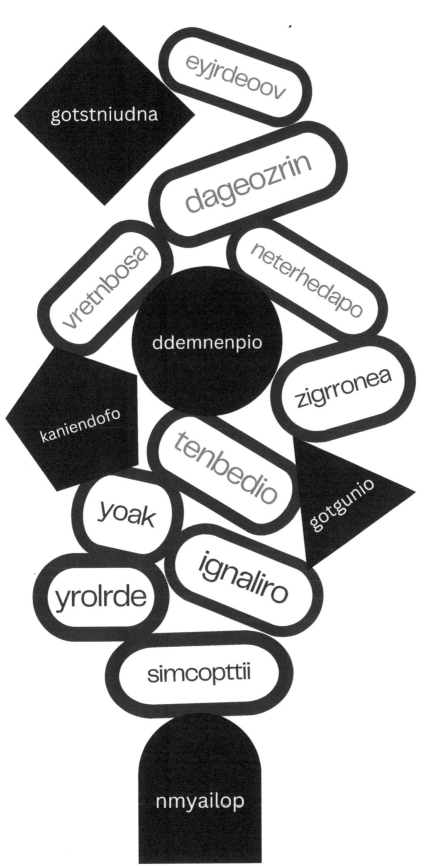

eyjrdeoov

gotstniudna

dageozrin

vretnbosa

neterhedapo

ddemnenpio

zigrronea

kaniendofo

tenbedio

gotgunio

yoak

ignaliro

yrolrde

simcopttii

nmyailop

obedient
observant
okay
olympian
oneofakind
openhearted
openminded
optimistic
orderly
organized
organizer
original
outgoing
outstanding
overjoyed

43

OBEDIENT

-submissive to the restraint or command of authority : willing to obey

OBSERVANT

-quick to notice things.

OKAY

-used to express assent, agreement, or acceptance.

OLYMPIAN

-very powerful, large, or impressive.

ONE-OF-A-KIND

-person or thing that is not like any other person or thing. Unique

OPEN-HEARTED

-someone who is honest, and generous and kind

OPEN-MINDED

-willing to consider new ideas, unprejudiced

OPTIMISTIC

-hopeful and confident about the future.

ORDERLY

-Orderly means neat, tidy, and well-organized

ORGANIZED

-having one's affairs in order so as to deal with them efficiently.

ORGANIZER

- person who arranges something (such as an event) especially by systematic planning and by coordinating the efforts of others.

ORIGINAL

-created ,not a copy or imitation.

OUTGOING

-friendly and socially confident.

OUTSTANDING

-very remarkable and impressive.having or showing grace or elegance.

OVERJOYED

-pleased ,Thrilled.. extremely happy about something

I   embody the following qualities:

Knowing yourself starts with thinking and expressing what is essential. Begin by stating your name and then affirm with "I AM."

- I am obedient and submissive to the restraint or command of authority : willing to obey

- I am observant and quick to notice things.

- I am okay with expressing consent, agreement, or acceptance.

- I am Olympian, mighty, large, or impressive.

- I am a one-of-a-kind person who is not like any other person. or thing. Unique

- I am open-hearted, honest, generous and kind

- I am open-minded and willing to consider new ideas unprejudiced.

- I am optimistic, hopeful, and confident about the future.

- I am orderly. Orderly means neat, tidy, and well-organized

- I am organized and have my affairs to deal with them efficiently.

- I am an organizer person who arranges something (such as an event) especially by systematic planning and by coordinating the efforts of others.

- I am created initially, not a copy or imitation.

- I am outgoing, friendly, and socially confident.

- I am outstanding, very remarkable, and impressive. having or they are showing grace or elegance.

- I am overjoyed, pleased , thrilled. pleased about something

New mindset, New directions, New
narrative, New creation,
NEW BEGINNINGS.....

In planning, I excel at orchestrating detailed organization to ensure seamless execution. Each project I undertake is distinguished by a unique touch that sets me apart. But what truly fuels my passion is social interaction, where I derive immense joy from spreading positivity and creating a vibrant atmosphere. My specialty lies in infusing events with inspiration and enthusiasm to bring joy and energy while sustaining an ongoing sense of excitement. My methodical approach involves strict adherence to guidelines with a keen eye for detail, akin to a vigilant observer. Maintaining a welcoming and upbeat demeanor, I am always ready to celebrate achievements with a high–five, fostering a positive and composed atmosphere. I embody a spirit reminiscent of an Olympian, radiating authenticity and standing out prominently in any setting. My intention is to be honest, kind, and unwavering in my determination to tackle challenges with an optimistic outlook, uncovering the best even in the face of adversity.

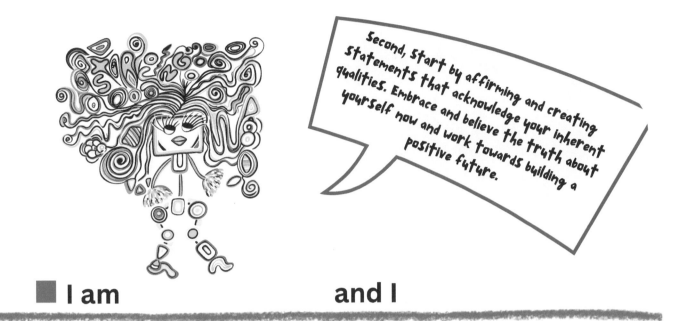

Second, start by affirming and creating statements that acknowledge your inherent qualities. Embrace and believe the truth about yourself now and work towards building a positive future.

■ I am   and I

_____

_____

_____

■ I am   and I

_____

_____

_____

I am   and I

Craft a declaration defining who you are presently or aspire to be in the future. Express your qualities, gifts, talents, and aspirations in this statement. Remember, there is always more to discover about yourself, so continue to write your vision!

I am _____ and I

I am _____ and I

I am _____ and I

I am   and I

I am   and I

I am   and I

I am   and I

BE STRONG

WHEN and WHERE you go each day

Each day, every day, and everywhere is the moment to practice and build your mental capacity. Regardless of whether you are in school, church, family, workplace, or an event, others misbehavior, such as unkindness and bullying, is not yours to accept or endure. These environments often concern individuals with low self-esteem, manipulation, and control issues. Usually, bullying behavior is someone who has been mentally hurt or physically hurt. And so controlling others around them is the answer when they can't control themselves. Most bullies are jealous, superior, and lack empathy. It can create fear within individuals, anxiousness, anxiety, health problems, lack of confidence, low self-esteem, and depression for those targeted.

Psychological, verbal, and physical bullying can be intentional assaults directly, spreading gossip and lies. These types of harassment and uncomfortable situations can also occur on the internet. No matter the situation, it is unacceptable. It leads to an increasingly alarming amount of mental illness and suicides each year. People should respect, inspire, encourage, empower, love, and be kind. It would help if you were mentally strong and did not allow this behavior into your life. Because it affects your social development during your early years and creeps into your adulthood. Never seek validation through people. The approval is needed only from you.

Reflection notes

"I can't is not an option...a TRY until you get it right."
Chris "Jayy" Johnson

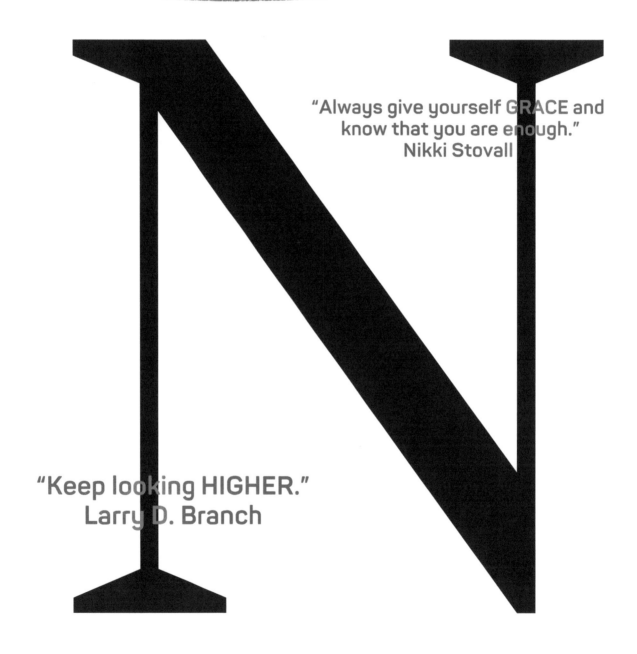

"Always give yourself GRACE and know that you are enough."
Nikki Stovall

"Keep looking HIGHER."
Larry D. Branch

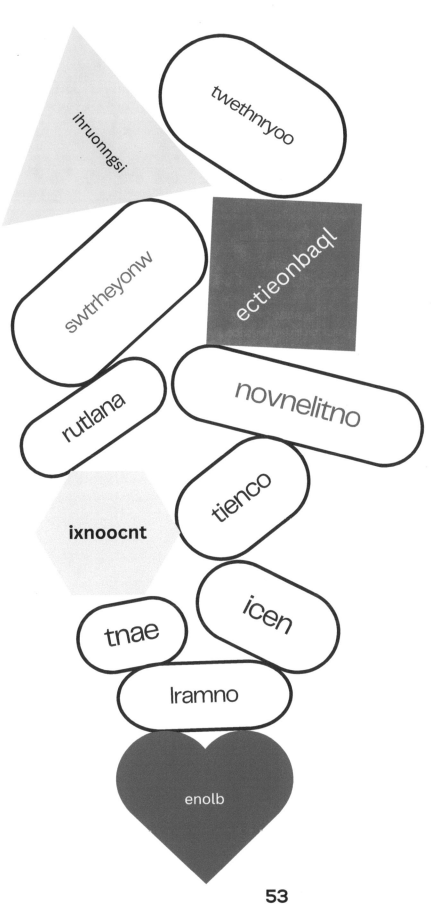

ihruonngsi

twethnryoo

swtrheyonw

ectieonbaql

rutlana

novnelitno

ixnoocnt

tienco

tnae

icen

lramno

enolb

natural
neat
newsworthy
nice
noble
noetic
nontoxic
nonviolent
normal
noteworthy
noticeable
 nourishing

53

NATURAL
-existing in or caused by nature; not made or caused by humankind.not artificial
Innate ability

NEAT
- done with or demonstrating skill or efficiency.arranged in an orderly, tidy way.

NEWSWORTHY
- interesting enough to be described in news report

NICE
-pleasant; agreeable; satisfactory.

NOBLE
- having or showing fine personal qualities or high moral principles and ideals.

NOETIC
-highly intelligent. Having to do with the mindNoetic comes from the Greek word
noēsis/noētikos, meaning inner wisdom, direct knowing, intuition, or implicit understanding.

NONTOXIC
- not poisonous or toxic

NONVIOLENT
- using peaceful means rather than force, especially to bring about political or social change.

NORMAL
-Conforming to the standard

NOTEWORTHY
- interesting, significant, worthy of note; deserving notice; outstanding; remarkable; notable

NOTICEABLE
- easily seen or noticed; clear or apparent.

NOURISHING
- containing substances necessary for growth, health, and good condition

Knowing yourself starts with thinking and expressing what is essential. Begin by stating your name and then affirm with "I AM."

I _____ embody the following qualities:

- I am natural, existing in or caused by nature; not made or caused by humankind, not artificial.

- I possess an innate ability and am neat, done with or demonstrating skill or efficiency, arranged in an orderly, tidy way.

- I am newsworthy and exciting enough to be described in a news report.

- I am friendly, pleasant, agreeable, and satisfactory.

- I am noble, having or showing fine personal qualities or high moral principles and ideals.

- I am netic and brilliant, and it concerns my mind. Noetic comes from the Greek word noēsis/noētikos, meaning inner wisdom, direct knowing, intuition, or implicit understanding.

- I am nontoxic, not poisonous or toxic.

- I am nonviolent, using peaceful means rather than force, especially to bring about political or social change.

- I am normal, conforming to the standard.

- I am noteworthy, interesting, significant, worthy of note, deserving of notice, outstanding, remarkable, and notable.

- I am noticeable, easily seen or noticed, evident or apparent.

- I am nourishing, containing substances necessary for growth, health, and good condition.

I embody a host of commendable qualities that make me a unique individual: I am noetic, characterized by high intelligence and a focus on the mind, encompassing inner wisdom, intuition, and implicit understanding. My lifestyle is nontoxic, devoid of harmful or poisonous elements, and marked by a commitment to nonviolence, utilizing peaceful social or political change methods. I adhere to expected standards while maintaining a productive demeanor. Noteworthy and easily noticeable, I am significant, outstanding, remarkable, and deserving attention. I provide the nourishment necessary for growth, health, and optimal condition. I am a natural force, inherently organized and efficient. My presence is newsworthy, leaving a lasting positive impression. I exude kindness, nobility, and high ethical standards, embodying exceptional qualities. Natural and untouched by human influence, I possess innate abilities and maintain neatness and efficiency in all endeavors. I am newsworthy, meriting description in news reports. Additionally, I am characterized by amiability, nobility, and a commitment to high moral standards.

Second, start by affirming and creating statements that acknowledge your inherent qualities. Embrace and believe the truth about yourself now and work towards building a positive future.

■ I am _____ and I

_____

_____

_____

■ I am _____ and I

_____

_____

_____

I am _____ and I

craft a declaration defining who you are presently or aspire to be in the future. Express your qualities, gifts, talents, and aspirations in this statement. Remember, there is always more to discover about yourself, so continue to write your vision!

I am _____ and I

I am _____ and I

I am _____ and I

I am   and I

I am   and I

I am   and I

I am   and I

The Importance of Taking the "For the Love of Humanity Pledge"

Maintaining a positive, healthy mindset is essential, and taking the Humanity pledge is a significant step in this direction. Cultivating love, kindness, respect, hope, knowledge, self-control, peace, and joy is critical. Do not allow yourself to become a victim of disrespect or bullying, but instead, have respectful boundaries for yourself and others and an anti-bullying mindset. Strive for personal growth in all areas and do not give up, nor consider suicide. You deserve self-love and respect from others and, most importantly, from yourself. So say no to self-condemnation and commit to self-love. Remember, the solution resides within you!

The humanity pledge involves acknowledging your worth, self-love, embracing your flaws, and prioritizing your mental and emotional well-being. By doing so, you not only improve your relationship with yourself but also with others. When you love and accept yourself, you radiate positive results and attract positivity in return. You become more confident, resilient, courageous, mentally strong, and compassionate towards yourself and others. So, take the pledge today and love yourself unconditionally daily. You are worthy of love and happiness; it all starts with self-love. Remember, you are the SOLUTION!

I PLEDGE

CERTIFICATE

I _____ PLEDGE

1.. TO BE MENTALLY STRONG

See everything in life as an OPPORTUNITY to learn and do better. When I do this, I will make the world a better place to live in because I am in it. This is how I will make a difference for humanity.

2. BELIEVE I AM MENTALLY STRONG

Everyone can tell you to believe. It will manifest in my life once I believe FIRST. I will continue to think about it, speak about it, apply action, and live the experience in my life. Starting TODAY!

3. BECOME MENTALLY STRONG

I will be consistent and continue to become mentally stronger by educating myself via self-development books, videos, peers, courses, family, and professional help if needed.

4. BE INTENTIONALLY COMMITTED

When having life CHALLENGES, agreeing or disagreeing with the outcomes is okay. I will apply a self-analysis and ask "What did I learn from the experience.? Afterward, apply the wisdom, knowledge, and understanding to move forward in a positive mindset. The goal is to achieve each task.

6. GOALS

Complete goals set in place. Adjust as needed

7. STAY FOCUSED

Decide that no matter what happens in life, I have options to advance me forward.

Welcome, and Congratulations!
To the "BE YOU" Creative Innovators Family!

"Never live in fear, live in FAITH."
Sir Gary L. Fulbright Jr

"Love YOURSELF the most."
Antoinette Lana Johnson

"Only one RACE and you
are the winner."
Roshanda D. Prior

tnlgee

tgare

sneugroe

giigvn

segiorraug

egeiunn

ulraomsgo

nsguie

tneloadrieog

nadrg

uetrlgaf

tfig

efdigt

neerstgsa

lboalg

egcra

generous
genius
 gentle
genuine
gift
gifted
giving
glamorous
global
goaloriented
gogetter
grace
graceful
grand
great
greatness
gregarious

GENEROUS
- showing kindness toward others , honesty and patience, and unselfishness

GENIUS
- A person who is exceptionally intelligent or creative, either generally or in some particular respect.

GENTLE
- having or showing a mild, kind, or tender temperament or character.
moderate in action, effect, or degree; not harsh or severe.

GENUINE
- not fake or counterfeit; original; real; authentic.

GIFT
-a thing given willingly to someone without payment; a present.natural ability or talent.

GIFTED
-having exceptional talent or natural ability.

GIVING
-providing love or other emotional support; caring.

GLAMOROUS
- full of glamor : excitingly attractive.

GLOBAL
-pertaining to the whole world; worldwide; universal.

goal oriented **GOAL ORIENTED**
- focused on reaching or completing specific tasks to achieve a planned outcome

GO-GETTER
- someone who is energetic and works hard to succeed

GRACE
- courteous; goodwill
simple elegance or refinement of movement.

GRATEFUL
- having or showing grace or elegance.

GRAND
- magnificent and imposing in appearance, size, or style.

GREAT
- an important or distinguished person.beyond what is ordinary or usual; highly unusual or exceptional or remarkable.

GREATNESS
-the quality of being great, distinguished, or eminent.

GREGARIOUS
-enjoys being with other people. marked by or indicating a liking for companionship

I _____ embody the following qualities:

- I am generous, show kindness toward others, and am honest, patient, and unselfish.

- I am a genius: A person who is exceptionally intelligent or creative, either generally or in some particular respect.

- I am gentle, having or showing a mild, kind, or tender temperament or character. moderate in action, effect, or degree; not harsh or severe.

- I am genuine, not fake or counterfeit; original, honest, authentic.

- I am a gift given willingly to someone without payment, a present: natural ability or talent.

- I am gifted with exceptional talent and natural ability.

- I am providing love or other emotional support and caring.

- I am glamorous, full of glamor, and excitingly attractive.

- I am global, about the whole world; worldwide, universal.

- I am goal-oriented and focused on reaching or completing specific tasks to achieve a planned outcome.

- I am a go-getter who is energetic and works hard to succeed.

- I am grateful and courteous, with goodwill, simple elegance, or refinement of movement.

- I am grateful for having or showing grace or elegance.

- I am grand, magnificent, and imposing in appearance, size, or style.

- I am a great impo,rtant, or distinguished person. beyond what is ordinary or usual; highly unusual or exceptional or remarkable.

- I am greatness, the quality of being great, distinguished, or eminent.

- I am gregarious and enjoy being with other people. Marked by or indicating a liking for companionship

65

New mindset, New directions, New narrative, New creation, NEW BEGINNINGS.....

I embody generosity by consistently displaying kindness, honesty, patience, and unselfishness. My productivity reflects genius, characterized by exceptional intelligence and creativity across various domains. I exhibit gentleness through a mild, kind, and tender temperament and moderation in actions, avoiding harshness or severity. Authenticity defines me as genuine, not counterfeit, but original and authentic. I possess the gift of natural ability or talent, making me gifted with exceptional skills. Furthermore, I am known for giving to nature, providing love and emotional support to others, and showcasing care and empathy. My demeanor exudes glamour, captivating with an exciting allure. I exist globally, with a worldview that transcends boundaries, embodying a universal perspective. Driven by goal orientation, I am focused on specific tasks to realize planned outcomes, embodying the spirit of a go–getter who works energetically to achieve success. Grace defines my demeanor by courteous goodwill and simple, elegant movement. I carry myself with grace and elegance, reflecting a refined demeanor. Grandeur marks my presence with a magnificent and imposing appearance and style. I embody greatness, transcending the ordinary to achieve exceptional and remarkable outcomes. Gregarious by nature, I enjoy the company of others, indicating a fondness for companionship and social interactions.

" BE YOU.... means be true to yourself by embracing and accepting your inside/outside beauty, both mentally and physically. The inside beauty is the joyful vibration of goodness, positivity, and self-love. The outside beauty is being unapologetic and proud of your attributes, features, talents, and your uniqueness without being influenced or defined by society. Live the best life by representing the one-of-a-kind masterpiece you were created to be."
Roshanda D. Prior

Strong people....
there is only one life
life is not forever on earth
they can, they will, they must at least TRY
to be intentional to fulfill destiny
no one has ALL answers
not to seek validation
not to compare
not to give up

SIDE

Discussing life from two different sides

BUILDING AND CONSTRUCTING YOU

NEGATIVE THOUGHTS THAT DESTROY YOU!

POSiTIVE THOUGHTS THAT EMPOWER YOU

Make goals this week for mental strength. Example Acts of kindness, positive thinking, eating healthy, exercise, keeping thinking of moooore!

Surround yourself around POSITIVE peers, family, friends that appreciate your PRESENCE.

Brain STORM

Imagine you were CHOSEN to create a version of YOU!
No limits. Think it, Say it, Become it. What is good and great about YOU?
(Example mind, heart, spirit, soul, body, etc

Continue to EXPLORE the BEST version of YOU!

Goals notes

Everyone is born with talents and gifts. What are yours?

Reflection Journal

Reflect on the day, jotting down what you're grateful for.
It's like a daily dose of happiness!
Practice, Self-compassion and tackle your fears one Step at a time.
Remember, every challenge is an opportunity to grow.

EXAMINING THE ART-BRAIN CONNECTION

When we immerse ourselves in art, our brains embark on a fascinating journey of perception and interpretation, with key brain regions taking the spotlight:

The Visual Cortex, situated at the back of our brain, processes visual elements like color, movement, and form.

The Frontal Lobe, our cognitive hub, contributes to conscious thought processes. It aids in the comprehension and contextualization of art by linking visual stimuli to our stored knowledge and experiences.

The Amygdala, responsible for emotions, plays a crucial role in emotional processing, enabling us to establish profound emotional connections with artwork.

Art and creativity are fundamental elements of human culture and personal expression. Just like the diversity within our species, art has always played a crucial role in various human societies, influencing and molding them. Art is a creative discipline showcasing the brain's Default Mode Network (DMN), the part that generates innovative ideas by connecting disparate pieces of information. We are all artists crafting our narratives through art's enduring and transformative influence. Each person is a masterpiece in progress, constantly creating and recreating within every daily endeavor.

Benefits of engaging in transformative visual arts and arts in education

-Increase independence
-Calmness, focus, and inner self-discovery
-Develop awareness of negative self-inflicted destructive thoughts
-Communicate more positive thoughts of hopes and dreams
-Provide a safe, creative outlet
-Focus and promote mental stretching
-Builds Fine Motor Skills, Neural Connections.
-Ability to make decisions that will enhance critical and problem-solving
  skills
-Healthy thinking creative stress management technique
-Discovered nonjudgment and acceptance
-Creative exercises help facilitate language development and
  communication connection
-Conscious and unconscious awareness
-Self-awareness introspective to examine healthy and unhealthy patterns
  of thinking, feeling, and experiences
-Develop talents and acknowledge strengths, some that have been long
  forgotten
-Encourage creativity, innovation, imagination, and self-confidence
-Creating ART stimulates dopamine production, providing us with a sense
  of motivation
-Decrease anti-social behaviors, foster a sense of community, enhance
  social skills, teamwork, and cultural awareness
-Help generate new ideas by connecting disparate concepts, which is
  central to creativity.

The process of creating and appreciating art plays a crucial role in shaping our BRAIN. It promotes brain plasticity, which is the brain's ability to form and reorganize synaptic connections. This, in turn, enhances cognitive flexibility and problem-solving skills, stimulating intellectual growth and engagement.

Objective

This transformative creative exercise aims to guide you through a journey of self-discovery and achievement from initiation to completion. By engaging in this interactive process, delve deep within yourself to activate, enhance, release, and address the voids you seek to fill. Embark on a voyage of self-exploration. Every individual is truly unique and incomparable. Be ORIGINAL and INNOVATIVE in this process. Attempting to mimic others is futile; the ultimate folly is yearning to be someone else while they aspire to be you. Each of us is a masterpiece, unparalleled. Mimicking another is like transforming a pineapple into a watermelon.

Often, internal conflicts arise from self-doubt, low self-esteem, lack of self-acceptance, anxiety, distorted thoughts, generalizations, frustration, and more. This creative method can aid in identifying, confronting, and initiating the process of overcoming these self-imposed limitations. Unresolved issues may lead to distress, but they do not define your narrative.

Self-improvement is an ongoing process of self-evaluation, introspection, and adaptation as we evolve, learn, and adapt to our changing environment. This transformative art exercise is a safe and natural way to help you process emotions and hormones you cannot release. Although medication is helpful and needed for some situations, there are some side effects. You have no side effects or overdosing from your own innate natural chemicals and hormones released via creative expression. RELEASE IT the natural way! This method is a visual unspoken language becoming a reality in art form.

Express your thoughts using various mediums, such as markers, inks, acrylics, pencils, colored pencils, pastels, and more.

Step One: **Initiate** with random lines.
Step Two: **Explore** with additional lines, numbers, letters, and shapes; no right or
 wrong paths exist.
Step Three: **Infuse** colors using the **different mediums listed below,** significant images, and overlapping to add depth. The overlapping will also create visual stimulation.
Step Four: **The primary focus is on the fundamental line structure starting from step two.** Delve further with letters, numbers, dates, and craft your unique symbols representing strength, aspirations, and dreams – the possibilities are limitless. Choose your choice of mediums such as inks, pencils, markers, colored pencils, acrylic, and spray paints etc. Some of these were used to create the original artwork in this book.

You can complete the transformative art quietly or with music. If you choose music, listen only to instrumental music, NOT lyrical music, because the words will guide your thoughts and may disrupt the subconscious creative flow. Discover new breathing patterns while connecting with your inner self in this judgment-free, limitless space where there is no right or wrong way.

Example of

Be You Creative Innovator Process.

This artwork was started simple with lines.
There is on wrong way. Be different.

The SOLUTION is within **BELIEVE.**

BEGIN   **KEEP BUILDING AND LAYERING**

FINAL

ADDITIONALCOMMERICIAL VERSION

LET'S BUILD!

Add, words, shapes, color, lines, symbols,numbers,There is no
wrong or right way. CREATE NEW AND UNSEEN

Reflective Questions:

- How did you feel during the creative process?

- Were you able to envision and think freely, without judgment?

- Did you allow yourself to be playful and unrestrained?

Let's continue! The sky isn't the limit! you are your ONLY limit! More of you is waiting create, recreate and "BUILD"

Name me _____

Example Victory, Joy, Hope, etc, etc

This puzzle is a word search puzzle that has HIDDEN FACTS ABOUT YOU REVEALED. First find all the words in the list. Words can go in any direction and share letters as well as cross over each other. Once you find all the words. Copy the unused letters starting in the top left corner into the blanks to reveal the hidden message.

BEAUTIFUL,BELIEVE, CONFIDENT, COURAGEOUS, CREATIVE, EXCELLENT, GIFTED, HAPPY, HEALTHY, HOPE, HUMBLE, JOY, KIND, LOVE, LOVEABLE, PEACE POSITIVE PRODUCTIVE, PROSPEROUS, QUALIFIED, SECURE, SMART, SUCCESS, UNSTOPPABLE

24 of 33 words placed.

```
U  G  I  F  T  E  D  B  H  B  E  D  L  I  E
N  T  V  E  Y  O  E  T  O  U  A  N  R  E  P
S  N  U  N  S  L  R  S  P  T  J  I  O  R  H
T  E  P  P  I  A  E  A  E  O  P  K  O  E  B
O  L  L  E  M  C  E  A  Y  O  N  S  A  L  D
P  L  V  S  U  C  C  E  S  S  P  L  Y  B  E
P  E  O  R  L  O  U  I  W  E  T  I  E  M  V
A  C  E  V  L  O  T  L  R  H  A  C  C  U  I
B  X  H  I  E  I  V  O  Y  E  V  E  A  H  T
L  E  A  L  V  L  U  E  V  I  T  A  E  R  C
E  Y  O  E  U  S  R  D  A  Y  R  E  P  A  U
L  U  F  I  T  U  A  E  B  B  P  M  S  L  D
C  O  N  F  I  D  E  N  T  S  L  P  H  R  O
S  U  O  E  G  A  R  U  O  C  K  E  A  J  R
D  E  I  F  I  L  A  U  Q  N  G  R  T  H  P
```

_____ ___ __

_____ ___ __

____ _____ __

___ _____

ANSWER KEY

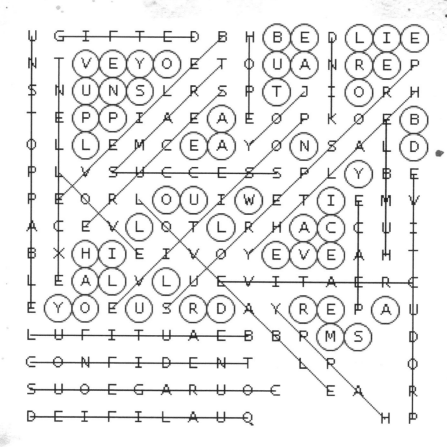

**BEAUTIFUL BELIEVE CONFIDENT
COURAGEOUS CREATIVE EXCELLENT
GIFTED HAPPY HEALTHY
HOPE HUMBLE JOY
KIND LOVE LOVEABLE
PEACE POSITIVE PRODUCTIVE
PROSPEROUS QUALIFIED SECURE
SMART SUCCESS UNSTOPPABLE**

Let's continue! Raise the bar, but with no restrictions!!
BE THE IMPOSSIBLE! Imagine more, streeetch and
"BUILD"

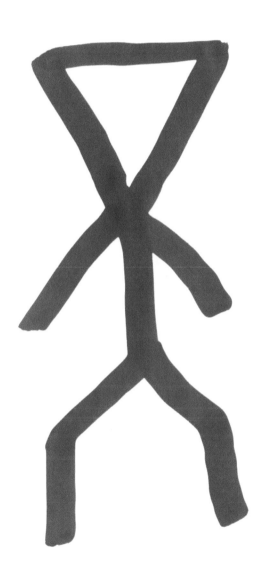

Name me _____
Example Freedom, Peace, Courage, etc, etc

About the author

Roshanda D. Prior, (1967– present) an eclectic contemporary Fine artist, entrepreneur, educator, art activist, author, and humanitarian. She was born and raised in Waco, Texas. Mrs. Prior has a degree in Business Administration, Bachelor of Fine Arts, and a Master of Arts in Art and cum laude graduate. She has traveled to Italy, France, England, New York, Washington DC, Georgia, California, Texas to explore Fine Arts. Mrs. Prior's love for life, nature, and different cultures via her art has inspired viewers. She states because of exploring oneself of mind, body, spirit, and soul, she has been able to challenge her creativity by combining unusual color palettes, lines, movement, and a variety of texture within her MASTERPIECE artworks.

Artist Statement

My eclectic contemporary style and creative expression capture layers of color, line, movement, and different textures. I am interested in creating mixed media distinctive art by collaborating found objects, metallic paints, different mediums, wood, metal, glass, and textiles. I have concluded the definition of the universe is one word... LIFE. Everything created must form, transition, and fulfill its purpose. To create as a result of what, when, where, and why is the question. Life is a transition through a process of ever-changing layers and fulfillment which only reveals itself when lived. Different art elements are repeated throughout each piece that is symbolic and meaningful regarding life transitions, the process, and the purpose of life. The entities of life are all beings and systems within the universe. The message "You are not the original creator of anything, only the passage way." Roshanda Prior

Entrepreneur

Roshanda D. Prior is the owner of the Protocol for Design LLC. Prior's vision is to create the world's leading company specializing in museum quality fine-art and distinctive décor for residential and commercial settings. Protocol for Design LLC's mission is to inspire, encourage, and invest in humanity worldwide. By providing the BEST selection of museum-quality original fine art, limited edition reproductions, and distinctive decor for residential and commercial settings, we are able to accomplish this mission for all art lovers, and fine art collectors. Our products are available EXCLUSIVELY online.

"CONFIDENCE"
!UO人EB Creative Innovators

REFERENCES

Winner, E., Hetland, L., Veenema, S., Sheridan, K., & Palmer, P. (2006). Studio Thinking: How Visual Arts Teaching Can Promote Disciplined Habits of Mind. In P. Locher, C. Martindale, & L. Dorfman (Eds.), New directions in aesthetics, creativity and the arts (pp. 189–205). Baywood Publishing Co.

Studio Thinking 2: The Real Benefits of Visual Arts Education
PUBLISHED: 2013
AUTHORS: Lois Hetland, Ellen Winner, Shirley Veenema, Kimberly M. Sheridan

Malchiodi, C. (2006). Art Therapy Sourcebook (2nd ed.). McGraw-Hill Professional.
200 more brief, creative and practical art therapy techniques : a guide for clinicians and clients
AuthorsSusan Buchalter(Author)
eBook2020
Eau Claire, Wisconsin : PESI Publishing & Media, [2020]

Ashley Bertsch's Podcast Episode:
https://www.youtube.com/watch?v=E3vcjqePr-U

Printed in the USA
CPSIA information can be obtained
at www.ICGtesting.com
LVHW070718180724
785647LV00002B/6